The Flying Lesson

by Virginia T. Gross

illustrated by
Gay W. Holland

Scott Foresman

Editorial Offices: Glenview, Illinois • New York, New York
Sales Offices: Reading, Massachusetts • Duluth, Georgia
Glenview, Illinois • Carrollton, Texas • Menlo Park, California

"Hatching is such hard work," Cobra complained. She knocked and pushed against her shell. Little by little the egg began to crack. Cobra grunted. She pushed and thumped and wiggled. At last the shell cracked open.

Cobra lay on the soft leaves, half in and half out of her shell. "Whew! I did it!" she muttered.

"Yes, and it's about time too," said a huge snake. Her eyes were brassy and glittering.

"Who are you?" gasped Cobra.

"I'm your mother, of course."

Cobra's mother coiled her dark body near the nest of leaves. She lifted her fine head and neck.

Cobra's eyes got big as she watched her mother. The big snake's hood spread from behind her head into a beautiful fan of ribs and skin. The sun shone through it, making it look like wings of light.

Cobra had never seen anything so lovely in all her life. But then, of course, she hadn't been living very long.

Cobra's mother uncoiled her long body. She began to slither away.

"Wait," called Cobra. "Aren't you going to teach me about the world?"

"You'll learn," hissed Cobra's mother. Off she slid into the evening.

"Oh," said Cobra. "I suppose I will." She coiled herself up in a circle. "I'll just stay here until someone brings me dinner."

A nasty little laugh echoed nearby. Cobra raised her neck and stretched her hood as she had seen her mother do.

"Who is there?" she demanded.

"Mongoose, that's who. And I'm laughing because you are about to be my dinner."

"You little pipsqueak," hissed Cobra. "Come out and fight. We'll see who gets dinner."

Cobra coiled tighter. She felt warm venom pushing through her cheeks. The poison rushed into her fangs. She felt very, very hungry. But Mongoose did not come out.

"Well," called Cobra. "Are you coming?"

"I can't," sighed Mongoose. "I'm stuck. You come here," he coaxed.

Cobra moved through the tall grass, looking for Mongoose. *Maybe I'm about to learn about the world*, she thought. Suddenly there was a swish and a fuss in the bush next to her tail. She turned. Tiny, sharp white teeth reached for her skin. Mongoose!

"Oh no, you don't!" cried Cobra. She rushed at the small bunch of fur.

"Wait!" squeaked Mongoose. "Let's work this out. Just help me get my foot out of this tangle. Then I won't eat you and you won't eat me. Okay?"

"I don't think so," Cobra answered. "I'm awfully hungry. And you're right here!"

Mongoose opened his mouth to argue. Then a noise, loud as a thunderclap, filled the forest.

"What's that?" shouted Cobra.

"It's only Hornbill," said Mongoose.

Cobra looked up. A bird soared from treetop to treetop. She dipped and glided. Her ivory beak caught the sun and glowed like fire.

"She's beautiful," exclaimed Cobra. "What is she doing?"

"She's flying. That's what hornbills do," said Mongoose.

"I want to do that," said Cobra.

Mongoose was about to insult Cobra. Then he had a better idea.

"Cobra," he chirped slyly, "if you get my foot out of this tangle, I'll help you meet Hornbill. She can teach you to fly."

Cobra imagined herself racing with clouds and wind. She turned her glittery eyes on Mongoose.

"How do I know you won't try to eat me when I set you free?" she asked. "And how do I know I can learn to fly?"

"Of course you can fly," laughed Mongoose. "You'll just have to trust me. That's what friends do, you know. Trust!"

His voice was very soothing.

"All right," Cobra agreed. But those little mongoose teeth were as pointy as daggers. "Close your mouth," she ordered.

She coiled her tail around Mongoose's neck, just in case. Then she began to untangle the tough vine with her fangs.

"Don't get any poison on my leg!" Mongoose cried. "It's sore enough now. I'll probably be lame for the rest of my life!"

Cobra soon freed Mongoose from the vine.

The two looked at each other. Both were hungry for dinner. But Mongoose was too lame to fight for it. And Cobra could think of nothing but her flying lesson.

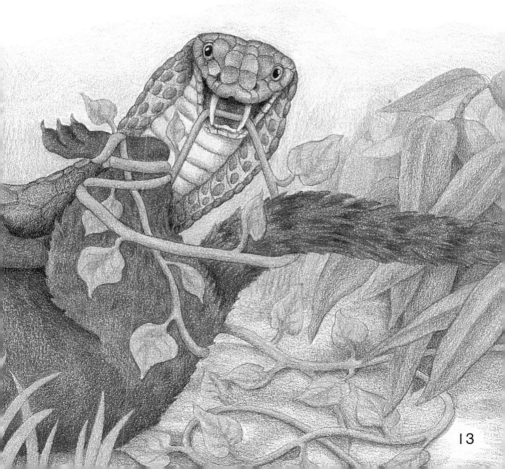

The next morning Cobra met Mongoose and Hornbill in the forest.

"Okay," Mongoose said. "Hornbill will teach you to fly."

Cobra coiled up in a tight ring. She swayed back and forth with excitement. She did not know about the bargain that Mongoose had made with Hornbill.

Soon this cobra would not be around to eat Hornbill's eggs. Soon the lame mongoose could have a cobra for dinner, without a fight. At least, that was the plan.

Two large claws picked up Cobra. Out and away they went. Higher. Higher!

Cobra squirmed. "Excuse me, Hornbill, but your claws are a bit prickly," she said.

"Then fly!" said Hornbill. She let go of the cobra. With a wail, the snake dropped out of the sky.

What a disaster! Cobra could not fly at all, for snakes were never meant to fly. Cobra was lucky this time. She landed in the large leaves of a rubber tree.

She learned a great deal about the world that day. She certainly learned never to trust a mongoose. And from that day to this, no cobra ever has!